THE AGE OF APOSTOLIC APOSTLESHIP SERIES

Preparations
for Ministry

PART **3**

On Behalf of
Connecting for Excellence
International Apostolic Network
CHURCHES AND MINISTRIES IN ASSOCIATION

By Dr. Alan Pateman

BY DR. JENNIFER PATEMAN

AVAILABLE FROM APMI PUBLICATIONS, AMAZON.COM AND OTHER RETAIL OUTLETS

THE AGE OF APOSTOLIC APOSTLESHIP SERIES

Preparations
for Ministry

PART **3**

DR. ALAN PATEMAN

BOOK TITLE: Preparations for Ministry
(The Age of Apostolic Apostleship Series) Part Three

WRITTEN BY Dr. ALAN PATEMAN
ISBN: 978-1-909132-60-3
eBook ISBN: 978-1-909132-61-0

Copyright 2017 Alan Pateman
Second Print/Update 2020

Published By:
APMI Publications
In Partnership with Truth for the Journey Books **21**
Email: publications@alanpateman.com
www.AlanPatemanMinistries.com

Acknowledgements:
Author/Design/Senior Editor/Publisher: Apostle Dr. Alan Pateman
Editing/Proofreading/Research: Dr. Jennifer Pateman
Computer Administration/Office Manager: Dr. Dorothea Struhlik
Cover Image Credit: www.PosterMyWall.com

Unless otherwise indicated, all scriptural quotations are from the HOLY BIBLE, NEW INTERNATIONAL VERSION ®. NIV ®. Copyright © 1973, 1978, 1984 by the International Bible Society. Used by permission of Zondervan Publishing House. All rights reserved.

*Where scriptures appear with special emphasis (**in bold**, italic or <u>underlined</u>) we have edited them ourselves in order to bring focused attention within the context of this subject being taught.*

❖

Table of Contents

❖

Preface

Over the years increasing numbers of men and women have been ordained and received impartation and anointing through this apostolic network.

To help them with their quest, God put a resolution in my heart that now is the time to put together teaching books that would not only help to prepare but would also help identify the seasons along the road to achieving maturity. Very often we think that God calls, we obey, He anoints and then we wonder why we're not in some dynamic, overflowing and internationally *recognized-by-all* ministry!

We need to understand that there is a process in God, not only of achieving maturity but also reaching that recognized place of success.

I believe through these foundation books *(part one, two, three and four)* of "The Age of Apostolic Apostleship Series," you will begin to understand and discover the many patterns regarding your failures or successes. Plus the reasons for those frustrated, unbelievably lonely periods when you begin to wonder whether you were ever really called at all.

You will discover that this is part of the road that one must tread to reach that fullness of maturity, which others will then recognize as being of God.

❖

Acknowledgements

Most of the credit for this book, "The Age of Apostolic Apostleship Series" **Preparations for Ministry** (Part Three), must go to all those I've been mentored by directly and those I've had the privilege to study their material and glean from, over many years.

It is impossible to grow into maturity without the knowledge and wisdom that comes from the impartation of others, through their dedication and relationship with God. Therefore you will find some sections from other writers; I hereby acknowledge their insight and challenging motivation and contribution.

Many thanks are not enough to express my appreciation to people like Ian Andrews, apostolic director of the International Association of Healing Ministries and the founder of Citadel Ministries; the late Reverend Dr. Bob Gordon whom I learnt so much from in my early years, who laid many solid foundations within my life; Dr. Roberts Liardon who has inspired me over the years to fulfil the apostolic call on my life; for Reinhard Bonnke, in seeing how an international organisation of great multitude is run.

Also Kenneth and Gloria Copeland who are both true witnesses of stature, unmovable faith and presentation; Dr. Robb Thompson who is an exceptionally skilled relational and leadership strategist. Dr. Bill Hamon for his leadership in bringing much needed truth, a father of the apostolic and prophetic movement. This list is endless, some I have known personally and others I have learned and watched from afar. These are true mentors. How we need fathers in the faith.

Finally: special big thanks to my wonderful wife Jenny. She is a true intercessor and Woman of God; she is truly bone of my bone and flesh of my flesh. For her practical help in guidance, typing and editing skills.

A ministry like this cannot exist without the practical support and the many prayers of those prayer warriors, which we call our partners.

Partners!
Thank you for your love and support.

❖

Introduction

This is the time of new beginnings especially as we have entered the New Millennium. Perhaps some might say, "Now is the count down for the Lord's return…" But the fact remains; there is much work to be done. We need stable, trained and Spirit led harvesters that are willing to go out into the harvest field.

The Call of God is to fulfil the Purpose of God

The call of God is not to be a good Christian only, is not to be successful in family life as an end in itself, is not to be successful in business pursuits, except it be the will of God. The call of God is to fulfil the purpose of God: "We are called according to His purpose." The purpose of God is made known to us through the knowledge of the mystery according to Ephesians 3:1-11.

We are called to be part of an apostolic company, to be joined together "in one accord," "of one heart and one soul" as the body of believers in Acts 1-4.

In these days the Lord is raising up apostolic companies, led by apostles with all the five fold ministries in place, to fully function as a body.

Each part of the body is "joined and knit together by what every joint supplies, according to the effective working by which every part does its share, causing growth of the body for the edifying of itself in love" (Ephesians 4:16 NKJV).

Apostolic Vanguard

Apostolic companies are the vanguard that God is raising up in these days to demonstrate to His people the victory He has given us over the devil. As apostolic companies begin to function in the fullness of our Messiah's authority in the earth, then a multitude of believers will flock to embrace the apostolic and the church will finally come to her destination, to rule and reign with Jesus our Messiah in Zion.

Paul Galligan from Revival Ministries Australia says, "The Pentecostal revival that began in the early twentieth century and has continued since was the restoration of the infilling or baptism of the Holy Spirit. It was not the restoration of the fullness of the Spirit of sonship. The Spirit of sonship is being restored today!

It is time for maturity, not time for Pentecost. Finally Pentecost is one of the foundations but sonship is the means by which the mature church reaches the destination, which is the glory of Christ revealed in His saints in the earth" (http://www.revivalministries.org.au)

It is our purpose therefore to provide instruction and training to:

- Understand the seasons we are in

- The heart of the fathers and sons (Malachi 4:6)

- Establish a solid foundation of faith

- Identify the area(s) of service to which the believer is called

- Help prepare him/her to serve actively under God and His leadership in the local church and community

LifeStyle International Christian University is a vehicle for these purposes. Our emphasis is not primarily academic, but practical. We aim to train believers through the practical application of biblical truths to life situations and to ministry tasks. The intent is that each student should become an asset to the local church, its leadership and its ministry purpose or vision.

❖

CHAPTER 1

Apostolic Pitfalls

Many abort their destiny by catching a glimpse of their future by running off in pursuit in the wrong season of development. They often quote God as being their strength, source and provision but they soon come to realise that something seriously is not working out. One becomes isolated, then discouragement hits.

Remember for these individuals, they have forsaken everything including the God given relationships that God intended to use to increase them. Of course they end up in the recycle tray waiting for God then to reconnect them so that they can get back on the road to what they regard as their destiny.

Fatherlessness vs. Fulfilment

Do we want to "father" when we have never been sons?
(John 8:38; Galatians 4:1-7)

Children, obey your parents IN the Lord, for this is right. "Honour your father and mother" – which is the first commandment with a promise – "that it may go well with you and that you may enjoy long life on the earth."
(Ephesians 6:1-3)

As I was thinking about the above scripture, it became obvious to me that for us who are in the ministry – *that there are many trying to be successful* - and yet not fulfilling the vision that is in their hearts. **I call this the pigpen mentality.** For many have wandered from their spiritual fathers, and decided to leave their spiritual homes *(churches)* and look to spend their spiritual inheritance *(anointing)* without a father's care.

This has resulted in frustration and discouragement. The *pigpen* is a place of shame and self-condemnation where no one is able to meet your need for love and intimacy. Who can fulfil that deep desire to be fulfilled with the intimacy that only can come from God? But this comes through spiritual fathers and mothers not even your natural spouse can fulfil that need.

Now when he had spent everything, a severe famine occurred in that country, and he began to be in need. And he went and attached himself to one of the citizens of that country, and he sent him into the fields to feed swine. And

*he was longing to fill his stomach with the pods that the
swine were eating, and no one was giving anything to him.*
(Luke 15:14-16 NASB)

It was not long after the son began to **_devalue_** the
relationship that he had with his father that he left his father's
house and began to seek wrong answers for right needs for
love and intimacy.

In a 1998 interview with Rick Knoth, managing editor
of the Assemblies of God Enrichment Journal, Promise
Keepers Founder and President Bill McCartney stated that
they had researched and found that 62 per cent of Christian
men admitted to struggles with sexual sin – pornography,
adultery and sensuality. When Christians value the Father
more for what He can do for them than for intimacy and
love, they eventually begin to seek to fulfil their own selfish
desires rather than walk in intimacy with God.

In order to fill the void that has been created, they may
begin to pursue one or more counterfeit affections – passions
of the flesh, power, possessions or position.

The question must be asked:

- Who is your spiritual father?
- Openness, transparency, and honesty: can you share
  these qualities with someone you consider your
  spiritual leader?
- Can you accept admonition and correction from them?
- Do you have a healthy relationship with a local
  church and its leadership?

- Who is your spiritual parent?
- Can you call yourself a daughter or a son?
- Whose child are you?

Without the spirit of sonship your inheritance is made very difficult. There's no comfort for the fatherless, only isolation and abandonment.

What is an Orphan Spirit?

Are you trying to earn acceptance, or can you rest in your sonship? Are you a servant who earns or the son who rests? Locate yourself, because servants lead like masters! Sons emulate their father's love. Intimate relationship is not necessary to those who seek only the *"position"* of leadership. Without this intimacy in relationship – abuse can occur.

Leadership operating in organizational authority void of relationship – leaves people feeling used, frustrated and induces rebellion.

Leading from the father/son perspective gives first place to relationship above protocol. "My son, I live for our relationship – where I can meet your needs, watching your growth and development. Go beyond my highest achievements and do more than I ever did." – A son watches his father and reproduces after the same kind. Careful not to grieve his father, the son will prepare himself with fidelity of heart, securing his inheritance.

From the son's perspective, he must be willing to lay down his dreams for the dreams of the father – trusting God for his inheritance.

Delinquent Fathers vs. Responsible Fathers

FATHER... Noun, *patër (πατήρ, 3962), from a root signifying* **"a nourisher, protector, upholder"** *(Lat, pater, Eng., "father," are akin).* Is used:

(a) of the nearest ancestor, e.g., Matthew 2:22;

(b) of a more remote ancestor, the progenitor of the people, a *"forefather,"* e.g., Matthew 3:9; 23:30; 1 Corinthians 10:1; the patriarchs, 2 Peter 3:4;

(c) one advanced in the knowledge of Christ, 1 John 2:13;

(d) metaphorically, of the originator of a family or company of persons animated by the same spirit as himself, as of Abraham, Romans 4:11, 12, 16, 17, 18, or of Satan, John 8:38, 41, 44;

(e) of one who, as a preacher of the gospel and a teacher, stands in a *"father's"* place, caring for his spiritual children.

The Function of "Nourisher, Protector, Upholder"

Moses summoned all the elders of Israel and said to them, "Go at once and select the animals for your families and slaughter the Passover lamb. Take a bunch of hyssop, dip it into the blood in the basin and put some of the blood on the top and on both sides of the doorframe. Not one of you shall go out of the door of his house until morning. When the Lord goes through the land to strike down the Egyptians, he will see the blood on the top and sides of the doorframe and will pass over that doorway, and he will not permit the destroyer to enter your houses and strike you down.

(Exodus 12:21–23)

This illustrates **the tremendous responsibility of being a father** because the *only* persons in Israel, who could obtain safety and salvation for their people, were *the Fathers of Israel.*

Derek Prince says, **"If the Fathers of Israel had been delinquent, Israel would not have been protected by the Passover."** And goes on to state, "the greatest single social problem that faces us, is delinquent fathers *[slack, neglectful and failing in duty]...* there are no delinquent children; there are only delinquent parents...

All the problems that we are concerned about, abortion drugs the break up of the family, many, many other social evils. I believe if you trace them to their source, their source is *delinquent fathers."*

I have pointed this out to you in this context, because if the fathers had failed; Israel would never have been redeemed. *God's plan depended on the fathers.*

Develop the Spirit of a True Spiritual Parent

True spiritual parents seek to raise up, promote, and send forth sons and daughters who will represent their heart to the nations *(1 Corinthians 4:14-16; 1 Thessalonians 2:7-12).*

True spiritual fathers prioritize relationship over performance, rules, and structure, although there is protocol.

Godly character manifests through a lifestyle of humility and love proved in relationship. Servant-leaders make decisions based upon the benefits and needs of others, not for themselves.

They launch forward into the nations spiritual sons and daughters *(remember discipleships, mentorship is not necessarily sonship)* by helping them to locate, develop and liberate their spiritual gifts and callings. Purity and holiness is the lifestyle outlived before all, having overcome worldly lusts, past hurts, disappointments and obstructions.

True spiritual fathers will provide:

- Security
- Unconditional love and acceptance
- Affirmation
- A sense of purpose and destiny
- Protection
- Role modelling
- Mentoring and equipping
- Responsibility and accountability
- Admonition and correction
- Inheritance – empowerment to go forth to the nations

The Hour is Desperate!

Scott Volk from Fire School of Ministry says, "I hear the younger generation crying out for 'spiritual fathers,' yet, when they're lovingly corrected and biblically rebuked by those very fathers, they write them off as being old-fashioned, traditional, and out of touch with what the Lord is doing in 'their generation.'

Maybe instead of fathers, they really want grandfathers who will simply pat them on the back, offering only grandpa-like encouragement and positive reinforcement.

I hear older men saying that they desire to be 'spiritual fathers,' yet, they're seemingly unwilling to get down in the relational trenches with the very ones that need to be fathered because their ministry schedules are too busy and they have more important things to do. Maybe instead of being spiritual fathers, they really want to be spiritual grandfathers who merely give a thumbs-up when ministry outwardly seems to be going well even though inwardly their grandchild may be withering inside.

Candy Grows on the Carpet

Why is it that children enjoy being around their grandparents? Could it be that at grandpa's house, where candy grows on the carpet and dessert is eaten instead of dinner, life is simply easier? Could it be because at grandpa's house, we can do almost whatever we please since grandpa is really not responsible for disciplining us; he merely desires to keep us happy until we return home?

I want to humbly confront both the generation that is crying out for fathers as well as the generation that says they desire to be fathers, with this simple challenge: it's time to step up to the plate. It's time that our words become something more than spiritual rhetoric. It's time for spiritual wayward sons to honour their fathers and it's time for spiritual dead-beat fathers to change their ways and assume the role that God intended them to have in their spiritual households.

We're living in a generation that is desperate to see the fulfilment of the Malachi 4 scripture that proclaims,

He will turn the hearts of the fathers to their children, and the hearts of the children to their fathers; or else I will come and strike the land with a curse.

It requires a turning on both parties – fathers *turning* to their children and children turning to their fathers. Now more than ever, when biblical standards are being compromised in the name of successful ministries, we need the fathers to lovingly put their arms around their children and guide them into all truth.

Now more than ever, as young people are being commissioned by the word of the Lord, we need to turn to the fathers, lest our youthful zeal and heavenly calling lead us into dangerous areas of pride and arrogance, eventuating in colossal failure and shame.

I believe we're at a desperate hour and that the Lord desires to seize it for His glory. Fathers, let's commit ourselves, by God's grace, to allowing our hearts to be turned to our children; children, let's commit ourselves, by God's grace, to allowing our hearts to be turned to our fathers.

Then and only then will the curse of Malachi 4:6 be avoided" (http://www.fire-school.org).

❖

CHAPTER 2

Promoting the Lord or Self?

There are certain individuals today who assume that they are in leadership when in actual fact they have never legitimately qualified for such position; rather born from ego and hidden agenda than the high calling of God!

People should think of us as servants of Christ and managers who are entrusted with God's mysteries. Managers are required to be trustworthy.
(1 Corinthians 4:1-2 GW)

So how do we recognise such individuals without starting a witch-hunt! Well they are really quite easy to spot but having said that, what is obvious to the trained eye is not necessarily obvious to the untrained and therefore spiritually vulnerable.

To begin with they are made up of the type of individuals who have for one reason or another been around the church world for many years and have a good grip on Christian "jargon" and "philosophy" yet more out of "head knowledge" and "learnt-behaviour" than from a genuine "living connection" with God! They come to believe that they have in some way been automatically chosen to be a *voice* to the church!

Qualifications and Insights

They even suppose that they have some sort of special "supernatural qualifications" and are convinced that they have some "special insights" that we all need - along with "special authority" to bring "correction" wherever they feel necessary - even to the entire body at large. So we must not fail to ask them, "Who are you and who has qualified you to be in such position?" Once they open their mouths they usually reveal themselves!

To keep things positive let's look at what qualifies a leader rather than what doesn't. According to scripture, there are two major qualifications for leadership.

- **First** of all there must be fruit; fruit of lifestyle and then fruit of ministry.

- **Secondly** there must be recognition and appointment *(see Acts 5:1-11; 6:1-7; Ephesians 4:11)*. But first we must look for the fruits; it's okay having a big mouth, but where is the fruit? Here are some scriptures concerning the "fruit of lifestyle" *(Galatians 5:22; Romans 12:3; 1 Timothy 3:1-f; Titus 1:5-16)*.

Consider our example in this matter; Paul the apostle, who went through years of "testing" once he submitted himself to the leaders at Antioch. *"They must first be tested; and then... let them serve..." (1 Timothy 3:10)* According to this particular scripture, once the "testing" part stops, the "serving" part begins! As Paul found out, this took considerable time.

It remains a fact today that in God's kingdom the way up is always down and the greatest amongst us is the servant of all. It is only the world that glories in arrogance and "ostentatious crowd-pulling" *(entertaining never qualified anyone for leadership!)*

Flamboyant or Humble

Someone with a servant's heart is not *showy or flamboyant* but humble. This is a good sign of leadership quality. In fact, for anyone who has genuinely been called to a leadership position within the body of Christ, one of **the first things that the Holy Spirit is going to deal with is *...ego!***

Yet as first mentioned above, certain individuals have the ability to "learn behaviour" that seems to be humble when in actual fact it is known as "false-humility." Perhaps we have become so familiar with the false that we no longer recognise the true. True humility is *often* misinterpreted.

Therefore we MUST be led by the Spirit, without Him we are spiritually dull and cannot see. We have eyes to see and yet cannot see; ears to hear but cannot hear. Only the Holy Spirit can REVEAL all truth to us and keep us spiritually alert *(John 16:13).*

He is the Father's complete provision for us - so that we cannot be so easily misled. But if we choose to walk without Him, to be vulnerable and spiritually ignorant, then no one can be blamed but ourselves! Yet we are meant to be "Over-Comers" in Christ, not gullible or easily led astray, but spiritual laziness is often the cause of dullness *(see apostasy).*

Now let us emphasise once again the fact that all potential leaders are "separated" or "set apart" by God *(it is never a **natural** selection; as seen in 1 Samuel 16:7)* and this "separation" actually means *"chosen."* Jesus Himself said, *"Many are called, but few are chosen..." (Matthew 22:14 KJV),* meaning that not many make it through the *"testing"* part! Yet the few who do are successfully "separated" unto the Lord *(so not everyone who claims to be a leader, is one!)*

While many want the name-tag of "leadership" not many want the "costs" or "associated risks!" And while the "separating process" was never intended to be easy, according to scripture, anyone caught "shortcutting" is not legitimate! *(John 10:7; Matthew 7:13)*

Offices and Positions of Service

There are "offices" and "positions of service" mentioned in the bible, *(1 Corinthians 12:28). "And God has appointed these in the church: first apostles, second prophets, third teachers, after that ... helps..." (NKJV)* Once again notice that during those first years in Antioch Paul did *not* occupy a "fivefold-office" *(see Ephesians 4:11)* but instead served in the ministry of helps, only then did he progress to the office of "teacher" *(see 2 Timothy 1:11; Acts 13:1).*

In Acts 13:1-2 we can see how Paul was listed along with other teachers in Antioch and how the Holy Spirit wanted them to be specifically "separated" unto Him. The appointed time had finally come, the one who had been called to be an apostle all those years earlier on the road to Damascus in Acts 9:15 had finally, after possibly 14 years of testing and loyal service, been successfully "separated" unto God to be an apostle.

First he was **"called"** then served in **"helps,"** then he progressed to the office of a **"teacher"** and finally the office of an **"apostle."** Why? The reason: Paul was faithful to promote the Lord and not himself *(see 1 Corinthians 4:2)*.

❖

CHAPTER 3

Your Destiny is Developed in Adullam

God has prepared a company of people with an anointing, to see breakthroughs in their own lives as well as in cities and nations. Many of these people are the most unlikely in the natural to be chosen by the Lord. How He loves to take the least likely and demonstrate His ability through them!

David was one of those "unlikely" people that God used to accomplish colossal breakthroughs. Just as the church is stepping into a new season, David came forth at a time when the Lord was transitioning His people from an old religious order *(Eli)* to a fresh new move of His Spirit *(David)*. Whenever God brings His people to a major juncture in history, He always raises up prophets to declare it.

The prophet Samuel stood at a major juncture in history and poured the anointing oil on young David. He declared a new authority was arising to defeat the powers of the enemy and release the will of God in the earth. "Then Samuel took the horn of oil and anointed him in the midst of his brothers; and the Spirit of the Lord came mightily upon David from that day forward..." *(1 Samuel 16:13 NASB)*

> *And such as do wickedly against the covenant shall he corrupt by flatteries: but the people that do know their God shall be strong, and do exploits.*
>
> *(Daniel 11:32 KJV)*

David's first Anointing

David received his **"first anointing"** in the midst of his own brothers. In an *obscure* place God chose an unlikely individual to accomplish great kingdom exploits *(Daniel 11:32)*. Unfortunately those close to David didn't embrace such an anointing on his life!

As with David, there are people who have known you in the old season of your life. Some of them will try to hold you to an old place, familiar to them. They want you to do the same things you did in the old season. They might enjoy your company but **don't want to go where you are going.**

After David received this "first anointing," he came face to face with the giant Goliath. **The enemy loves to challenge the new anointing in your life.** He doesn't want you to move forward. However, war was not new to David. He had defeated the lion and the bear during the old season. Now he faced the enemy that was resisting David's destiny. An incredible courage rose up in David as he asked the question, "Is there not a cause?" *(1 Samuel 17:29 KJV)*

David was not in the battle for his own benefit. He realized there was a cause at stake, the advancement of God's kingdom in the earth. Those who will be part of the Davidic Company that God is raising up in this hour must be free from fears and selfish interests. It is a time when fears must be replaced with great courage! During this time, we must deal with insecurities, intimidation, limitations, and jealous spirits. All of these are designed to keep this Davidic Company from God's destiny.

After David's "first anointing," he ended up in a dark place. "So David departed from there and escaped to the cave of Adullam; and when his brothers and all his father's household heard of it, they went down there to him" *(1 Samuel 22:1 NASB)*.

Darkness, Obscurity and Confusion

Adullam was a place of darkness, obscurity and confusion. God's future generals often find themselves in obscure places. However, in the dark place of Adullam, David found a place of prayer. **As the seed of destiny dies, we learn that God is our only hope.** In the times of weakness, the Lord becomes our strength *(2 Corinthians 12:9)*.

During David's hour of unpopularity, he discovered whom the people were that would stand with him. Real friends are committed to you in the good and the hard times. Only those who have true heart connections will stand with you in difficult days. The body of Christ is in a time when we will know those whose hearts are knitted to our hearts.

God gathered around David those who were discontented, and those in debt *(1 Samuel 22:2)*. From a small number of unlikely people, God brought forth from the cave a powerful army of 340,000 recruits! The hidden place became a place of multiplication.

Second Anointing and Praise

Today, God is assembling His army. God's Army is made up of those generals who have been in a hidden place in the last season. Their hearts have been knitted together to see King Jesus exalted in the earth. They have come forth with the anointing at Judah. David received his **"second anointing"** at Judah. Judah means praise. **Praise will be a key to victory.**

The seed of destiny in these lives that seemed dead is coming forth now in resurrection life and power! David received his **"third anointing"** at Hebron. Hebron was a place of alliance. It was the place of making commitments, entering relationships and cutting covenants. As a result of these alliances, David and his army was able to take back ground the enemy had stolen.

They were able to declare that God is the God of the Breakthrough. "So David came to Baal-parazim and defeated them there; and he said, *'The Lord has broken through my enemies before me like the breakthrough of waters.'* Therefore he named that place Baal-perazim" *(2 Samuel 5:20 NASB)*.

God is gathering a powerful group of people in these days. Lives are joining together in covenant relationships. Ministries are aligned to see the kingdom of God advance through the earth. Many of the ministries have been in Adullam in the past season. However, they are being properly aligned so the seed of destiny in them is released to accomplish great kingdom exploits.

Destiny has a time for fulfilment. **Great courage will be needed as we embrace our destiny.** These are days when we will see new enemies. Old war strategies and independent spirits will not be able to stand against these enemies.

A synergistic alliance of powerful visionary ministries is emerging as a Davidic Army for the new season. They are anointed for powerful breakthrough in cities, territories and nations. Their testimony proclaims, *"Jesus is God of the Breakthrough!"*

❖

CHAPTER 4

The Strength of the Anointing

The Bride of Christ, can she handle the strength of her own anointing? Are we fighting the Holy Spirit and not even aware of it...? "Against You, You only, have I sinned" *(Psalm 51:4)*.

Can we contain and understand the season that we are in? Some time ago, I was watching **Billy Brim** on TV in the UK, who was being interviewed in front of a live audience. They were discussing the anointing of the last days to be poured out upon the body of Christ before Jesus returns.

Mention was made to the effect that if the Lord had poured out the kind of anointing upon the church that He plans to before Christ is able to return, then it would most certainly have wiped many people out because the church is still not yet adequately prepared.

People have to be brought to that place where they can handle the anointing and it not kill them, as in the case of Ananias and Sapphira *(Acts 5:5)*.

People aren't going to get away with some of the things they may have got away with up to now in the church. **The apostolic anointing is currently being restored to the church with the strength of the anointing that existed on the apostles in the early church.** If people come against that anointing they will find themselves fighting the Holy Spirit.

I believe this apostolic move of the end times will restore the true FEAR OF GOD back into the church. To be found fighting, resisting or even lying to almighty God is never good! And when we do find ourselves in that position, we usually cause ourselves much unnecessary harm!

Sin directed against the Holy Spirit

David possessed such revelation, as seen in Psalm 51:4 where he is quoted as saying to the Lord, **"Against thee, thee only, have I sinned"** *(KJV)*. This helps to reveal that when Ananias and his wife *lied,* such sin was not directed against the apostles but against the very person of the Holy Spirit. Just think how many people sin against the Holy Spirit and don't even recognize it!

However in their particular case, I do personally believe that the purity of the Holy Spirit and the wickedness of their own hearts caused such a conflict inside of them that it killed them. They could not stand in the presence of a Holy God and we must understand that this sort of thing may begin happening again, as part of the restoration of the apostolic.

*O worship the LORD in the beauty of holiness: **fear** before him, all the earth.*

(Psalm 96:9 KJV)

There must be **holiness** in the body of Christ. Jesus is coming back for a bride without spot or wrinkle and without adultery in her heart for the world and her beauty will be as the scripture says, **"...the beauty of Holiness."** While there are *many* unclean spirits in this world, there is only one **HOLY** Spirit!

The nations once again will posses a fear for the children of God, for the **true unadulterated power in the church of the end times.** Just as in the days of the early church, God will display His power through the apostolic ministry. Even though many will be unprepared and not able to handle such an anointing, it MUST be intensified *(the anointing that is)* before Jesus returns.

Billy Brim continued, **"...as much as the anointing is powerful to create, it is as powerfully destructive of evil."** Holiness will show up wickedness in the hearts of men.

Think of it like this, when Jesus turned the water into wine at the wedding feast, what kind of powerful reaction went on inside of those jars *(atomic)* and yet it didn't shatter them! **We as the church have got to be able to contain the anointing without it shattering us!**

Resisting the Anointing

To grieve the Holy Spirit is a serious offense and not something to be taken lightly. Apostles are human vessels chosen by God - capable of making mistakes - but the anointing they carry is sacred. God carefully prepares them and we can see this if we carefully study the lives of Paul and the other apostles.

Many end time apostles are walking the earth again, so dead to self, so yielded to obeying Jesus and so perfected in the love walk that the authority they have is unparalleled. Nations are listening to them because God has granted them a genuine "VOICE" that can be heard.

Apostles are greatly opposed but they have the anointing and the help of the Holy Spirit to handle it. *The world is not worthy of them!* The world reacts to them in every way. They live in a perpetual position of vulnerability and yet of great influence! As we saw with Paul, he was never free of temptation or trials but was a powerfully anointed vessel that carried holy *revelations* directly from almighty God.

Don't Kill the Apostle

In the end times, people will carry such anointing, as we have never seen before. **Many will fail to understand and even become "offended."** The reality is that most people don't know how to recognize true anointing; therefore many will find themselves resisting God in these days!

People found themselves wanting to kill Paul without any concept of who or what he really was. They often rose up in violent opposition against him, but were completely ignorant of the true presence and force of God within him. Everywhere he went somebody or something wanted to kill him! So we must not be surprised at the violent reactions that some people will experience - especially when they come up against this apostolic anointing in the wrong way.

Saying, Touch not mine anointed, and do my prophets no harm.

(1 Chronicles 16:22; Psalm 105:15 KJV)

David had a revelation about not touching God's anointed. Even when tempted to *retaliate,* he always resisted. When Saul's behaviour was at its worst, David still recognized the anointing that was upon his king and would not touch Saul. *(This is a healthy **none-negotiable** for us all!)*

During the famous encounter in the cave that Saul visited in order to *relieve* himself, David had the perfect opportunity to kill or capture Saul. He could have said, ***"Oh Lord... thank you for finally delivering this wretched man into my hands!"*** Instead David did *not* judge the situation by the standards of his flesh but by the revelation of God in his heart, concerning the anointing. Oh how we need this revelation in the church today.

Be Found Walking

It's no small thing to be found resisting or grieving the Holy Spirit. Even though we are heirs of salvation and have the revelation of Jesus Christ, we must still be found walking with the Holy Spirit and by His holiness, especially in these last days!

The world needs to see the church living and walking in the miraculous supernatural power of the resurrection.

But I say, walk and live [habitually] in the [Holy] Spirit [responsive to and controlled and guided by the Spirit]; then you will certainly not gratify the cravings and desires of the flesh [of human nature without God].

(Galatians 5:16 AMP)

CHAPTER 5

Humanism vs. The Spirit of God

I warn everyone who hears the words of the prophecy in this book: If anyone adds anything to this, God will strike him... If anyone takes away any words from this book of prophecy, God will take away his portion of the tree of life... *(Revelation 22:18-19 GW)*

Admittedly this focus on "leadership seduction" may seem slightly negative, but a subject that must be addressed nonetheless and always better tackled than left. After all, a lot of us have encountered these types of people who either don't want to change or are completely ignorant that anything is wrong.

Nevertheless we still have the option of heaping up many teachers to tickle our ears as scripture puts it, with tastefully designed and politically correct teachings that only address what we want to hear. Yet avoiding all things negative is not wise and keeps us shallow and uninformed. Awareness *(not conspiracy theory)* prevents spiritual threats, which arrive on the doorstep of *every* church group or ministry. No one is immune; *ask me how I know!*

So to continue, yes - bogus leaders without qualification or recognition hate to be challenged; yet challenge is precisely what reveals their false anointing. They are easily threatened. True anointing attracts trouble, it comes with the territory. But these individuals have a hatred for all things *"challenge"* or *"change"* because they reveal insecurity and weakness like nothing else.

I believe that the Holy Spirit uses change in order to teach us, and sometimes it may even seem that the only "constant" in life is change! It keeps us fresh and unstuck. Change is not synonymous with crisis as some folks treat it. And it helps to keep in mind that our behaviour in the first moments of a crisis reveals who and what we truly believe.

Character Assassination is another Trait

Many of us have had our integrity questioned and it's never pleasant. Generally it doesn't stop with us either but also affects our families, our marriages and every area possible... *(Especially if we are leaders)*. However it is the accuser of the brethren who does this. But there is balance to everything and leaders must not use this as a clock to cover everything by saying, *"...don't question me about anything..."* No! We must remain accountable to our flock, to each other and to the word.

Bogus leaders never enhance unity and leave a trail of separation and disunity in their wake, of marriages, associates, and friends; even longstanding relationships, all left in tatters (see Proverbs 16:28). They don't co-habit and when they have the opportunity they specialize in rescuing and then despising!

Falsehood, *(2 Corinthians 11:4, 26).* The bible speaks of many falsehoods such as false brethren, false apostles, false spirits, false doctrines and false prophets, to name a few. The point is this, **there is a counterfeit to anything that has an original!** For example we never get to see counterfeit $30 dollar bills or £9 pound notes, simply because there was never an original!

Uncanny ability to Misread

False brethren for instance are those who consistently find something to make an accusation about. They are not unlike false witnesses except they shout about stuff they do witness but don't like! And there's nothing much they do like! The humanism that steers them is not of the Spirit of God; they have the uncanny ability to totally misread everything!

They easily make a controversy over anything and seek to correct their leaders by saying, *"We don't want to undermine you, BUT..."* Usually these same people have such delicate consciences (no faith) that they use this to manipulate their leaders to pass everything by them first; to the effect that nothing happens without their approval!

What all these people struggle with - is *humanism* - more often than not they exalt psychology, science of the mind rather than the very word of God. In fact false leaders love to quote more from their psychology books than from scripture; yet quote just enough scripture to keep it convincing! They offer a complete mix. Mixing the word with anything is dangerous, because it must be kept pure, unadulterated and defined as the true word of God.

Even though psychology has its place, though limited, it certainly must not be mixed with the word of God; especially where people don't know the difference! To qualify this let me say the following: If people insist on using psychology, they must define it as such and not mix it with - add it to - or - mistake it for - the word of God, because pretty soon people in general won't be able to recognise the difference.

The Mind in its Fallen-State

Besides - psychology only applies to the "fallen mind" not to the "renewed mind." Those born of the Spirit know their mind is being renewed by the word of God daily. Psychology only studies the mind in its fallen-state but it cannot renew anything! Humanistic reasoning's must not be added to God's word (see Revelation 22:18).

Clearly not everyone who claims to be genuine and led by the Spirit is what they say they are. However scripture gives us one main source of evidence to prove or disprove the genuine from the bogus - "FRUIT." Its presence or absence speaks volumes. If any of us truly walk by His Spirit, there will always be evidence to prove it! There is always evidence to the life of the Spirit. Tongues for example is evidence of the baptism, fruit is the evidence of the Spirit led life. Whether it is fruit of character or of ministry, there is *always* fruit where the Holy Spirit resides.

Finally, even though we have looked into the behaviour of the false and bogus - none of this is personal or aimed at flesh and blood, rather spiritual forces that are opposed, hostile or anti-Christ (anti-anointing, anti-truth, anti-righteousness!) The anointing breaks every yoke of bondage, which takes genuine authority!

Remember that where the counterfeit can only question Christ, the true anointing reveals Him.

❖

CHAPTER 6

Divination
and the Python Spirit

Felt under spiritual attack lately? Well here's a passage that helps describe the kind of spiritual attack we've all been experiencing.

As we were on our way to the place of prayer (church), we were met by a slave girl who was possessed by a spirit of divination (python - see KJV) [claiming to foretell future events and to discover hidden knowledge], and she brought her owners much gain by her fortunetelling. She kept following Paul and [the rest of] us, shouting loudly, These men are the servants of the Most High God! They announce to you the way of salvation! And she did this for many days. Then Paul, being sorely annoyed and worn out, turned and said to the spirit within her, I charge you in the name of Jesus Christ to come out of her! And it came out that very moment.

(Acts 16:16-18 AMP)

Firstly notice that this was not a spirit of stealth and seduction but of harassment and pestering torment. Divination or python, exposes, provokes, discredits, humiliates and even bankrupts. Notice how it did not just target Paul but his entire apostolic company, "...she kept following Paul **and [the rest of] us,** shouting loudly."

Unpleasant Mental State

Folks, as part of Christ's apostolic company (see Hebrews 3:1 KJV) we too are the targets for such harassment, designed to sorely annoy and wear us out. We know this because it goes on to say, "She did this for **many days.** Then Paul, **sorely annoyed and worn out** turned and said..." According to the dictionary the word "annoyance" refers to an unpleasant mental state that is characterized by such effects as irritation and distraction... and can lead to emotions such as frustration and anger. It refers to the act of making unwelcome intrusions upon another.

The Greek for "grieved" as used in the King James Version (instead of annoyed) means: "to manage with pains, accomplish with great labour; to be troubled, displeased, **offended**, pained and **to be worked up**" (Strong's #G1278).

Perhaps Paul was not on best form after "many days" of such annoying harassment. Plus the original language confirms that it was just "a young female slave" who got under his skin *(annoyed him so much!)* Her masters weren't interested in harassing Paul - there was no money in it for them - she even lost them money. Instead she locked target with Paul *(and the others)* and wouldn't let go - until Paul put an end to it.

Never Take Spiritual Warfare Personally

What's puzzling is, why did Paul take so long to respond? I would suggest to you, that the devil wants us to react to everything and to take *everything* personally. Paul on the other hand knew that she was just a "servant girl." I want to remind you, that it's never a good time to take things personally; especially in spiritual warfare, we are all prone to this! It's hard sometimes because the devil uses people.

Still this spiritual-struggle that we are in, is never against *people.* "Our struggle is **not against flesh and blood,** but against the rulers, against the authorities, against the powers of this dark world and against the spiritual forces of evil in the heavenly realms" (Ephesians 6:12 NIV; John 17:14-16 KJV).

Once we start taking things personally, we have lost the plot completely. Self-preservation makes us lose our focus and our purpose (Christ's agenda was never self preservation). Self-preservation - always motivates us - out of the will of God. We become defensive and our sensitivity to God becomes seriously impaired. All spiritual warfare is targeted at Christ (hence anti-Christ) and is therefore never personal. (Remembering this fact can really help prevent the roots of bitterness - see Hebrews 12:15).

However we know that Paul was capable of being led of the Holy Spirit, because of preceding events mentioned earlier in the same chapter. At each major juncture of their travels, we see an interaction between Paul and his apostolic company and the Holy Spirit.

For example it says in the passage below that, "...**they** were **forbidden by the Holy Spirit** to preach the word in Asia" (right place - wrong time). We also know that Paul was quick to respond to the Holy Spirit's guidance because it says also, "Now after he [Paul] had seen the vision, *immediately* **we** sought to go to Macedonia, **concluding that the Lord had called us to preach the gospel to them.**"

> *Now when they had gone through Phrygia and the region of Galatia, they were **forbidden by the Holy Spirit** to preach the word in Asia. After they had come to Mysia, they tried to go into Bithynia, but the Spirit **did not permit** them. So passing by Mysia, they came down to Troas. And a vision appeared to Paul in the night. A man of Macedonia stood and pleaded with him, saying, "Come over to Macedonia and help us." Now after he had seen the vision, **immediately** we sought to go to Macedonia, concluding that the Lord had called us to preach the gospel to them.*
>
> *(Acts 16:6-11 NKJV)*

So this apostolic company, who were "forbidden" by the Spirit, also knew to "conclude" when they were permitted to preach the gospel in Macedonia. They knew how to be led by the Holy Spirit. With this in mind, are we to believe they missed it, when it came to a mere "servant girl"?

Did Paul (who responded immediately) suddenly become delinquent? Either Paul concluded deliberately to ignore her for many days, then out of mere exhaustion succumb to the frustration of relentless spiritual harassment (Moses also struck the rock twice out of frustration with the people and suffered the consequences). Paul - waiting on the unction of the Holy Spirit (to minister deliverance) only delayed his response - out of a knowledge of the spiritual climate and what sort of trouble it would stir.

When we read accounts like this in the bible, there was so much going on. Our lives are much the same. It takes great discernment to distinguish what's really happening. On a human level, we've all been annoyed and worn out (especially in the ministry!) So whether Paul acted out of frustration and spiritual exhaustion or not, the servant girl was still delivered and Paul's jailer (and household) were saved!

More than Conquerors

Many other miracles occurred also, and I would suggest, that it was because Paul faced and did not run from spiritual warfare. (He knew about Daniel 7:25 and how it was the enemies ploy to wear him out).

The consequences might have seemed heavy, but what were the alternatives, to do nothing or pursue and recover all without fail like David did in 1 Samuel 30: 1-19? If we just lick our wounds we'll lose everything.

However we are more than conquerors, we triumph through Christ, who is greater in us, than he that's in the world! (Romans 8:37; 2 Corinthians 2:14; 1 John 4:4 KJV paraphrased).

❖

CHAPTER 7

A Work of Sovereign Grace

We are going to be looking at the "grace" needed for our "appointment." Chiefly looking at the life of Paul the apostle, we see that he too needed grace to do what he was appointed to do.

Having gifts (faculties, talents, qualities) that differ according to the grace given us, let us use them.
(Romans 12:6-8 AMP)

So to begin with, the most important fact to remember is that the call-of-God is actually a working of His sovereign-grace, sovereign – because it is His choice to make and His alone! In other words, God does not always call the most likely or the most naturally talented! In fact His choosing is rarely ever popular and all mystery concerning His "calling" or "election," can only be answered within the very heart of God (1 Corinthians 1:27-29).

However as our opening scripture states and as the NIV continues it says, **"We have different gifts, according to the grace given us.** If a man's gift is prophesying, let him use it in proportion to his faith. If it is serving, let him serve; if it is teaching, let him teach; if it is encouraging, let him encourage; if it is contributing to the needs of others, let him give generously; if it is leadership, let him govern diligently; if it is showing mercy, let him do it cheerfully" (Romans 12:6-8).

Gift Discernment

A major weakness concerning our "gift-discernment" tends to have been our lack of understanding concerning the "responsibility" that is involved in our election. In this respect then, natural talents don't add up too much when answering the specific call of God!

This is where stewardship comes into it, as we see Paul mentioning here in 1 Peter 4:10 (AMP) "As each of you has received a gift (a particular spiritual talent, a gracious divine endowment), employ it for one another as [befits] **good trustees** of God's many-sided grace [**faithful stewards** of the extremely diverse powers and gifts granted to Christians by unmerited favour]."

Granted this is a bit of a mouthful in the Amplified and is perhaps better when more simply put, as here in the Authorised Version, "as every man hath received the gift, even so minister the same one to another, **as good stewards of the manifold grace of God**" (KJV).

Nevertheless we see in both these respected versions of the bible the use of the word "steward." God has simply called us to be good-stewards of His grace (authority and ability). Notice we are not stewards of just anything - but specifically of His grace.

To help us define this word steward a little better, let me say the following, **the biblical doctrine of stewardship defines a man's relationship to God. It identifies God as owner and man as manager.** God makes man His "co-worker" in "administering" all aspects of our life. The apostle Paul explains it best by saying, "For we are God's fellow workers; you are God's field, God's building" (1 Corinthians 3:9 NASB). This helps us to better evaluate our position in this life.

Stewardship Defines our Purpose

In essence then, stewardship defines our purpose in this world - as assigned to us by God Himself. It is our divinely given opportunity to join with God in His worldwide and eternal redemptive movement (Matthew 28:19-20). In truth, stewardship is not God "taking" something from us, rather it is His method of bestowing His richest gifts upon His people.

I suggest that the following words best describe this concept of "stewardship" as seen in scripture: manager, foreman, guardian, governor, procurator and administrator (see Galatians 4:1-2 AMP). In fact we see this more contemporary word of "manager" specifically in the "God's Word Translation" of the bible where it says, **"Each of you as a good manager must use the gift that God has given you to serve others"** (1 Peter 4:10 GW).

Clearly then, our faithfulness in managing God's affairs exceeds the traditional boundaries of just managing finances correctly or faithfully paying our tithes and offerings! Paul likens his own calling to that of an "administrator" or "steward" of God's grace. He viewed God like the master of a great household who wisely administrated His affairs through Paul - an obedient servant of Jesus Christ (see Ephesians 3:2 and 1 Corinthians 9:17).

To continue with our focus on **"grace,"** however it is important to notice how often this word "grace" is actually used by Paul in the scriptures: "The **grace God gave me** to be a minister of Christ Jesus" (Romans 15:15-16); "They recognise **the grace given to me**" (Galatians 2:9); "I became a servant of this gospel by the **gift of God's grace** given me" (Ephesians 3:7); "Assuming that you have heard of the **stewardship of God's grace** (His unmerited favour) that was entrusted to me [to dispense to you] for your benefit" (Ephesians 3:2 AMP).

The Grace Given

I believe that Paul constantly referred to "the-grace-given-to-me," simply because he was overcome by the fact that God had not only put **"grace"** into his life, but more specifically **"a-grace"** into his life. There is a difference! The specific "grace" that God had given to Paul literally controlled and directed his entire life. We see this clearly in Romans 12:3 where he says, "For **by the grace given me** I say to every one of you."

Incidentally - speaking by the grace God had given to him – did not refer to a special eloquence of speech. No! But something far more potent – which was the very "authority" of God! Gracious speech had nothing to do with it; but the "authority-by-which-he-spoke" was the key.

The grace of God refers also to the gift of God, which was given to Paul for his life and ministry – that also warranted him the authority he needed to administrate on God's behalf. Therefore grace can quite simply be seen as the "authority" and the "ability" of God in our lives. Given to us to benefit others and to "manage" God's affairs on His behalf.

Finally, this was Paul's motivation. He knew what the grace was. He identified the grace within his own life. He understood that he was both called "by-grace" and called "into-grace." The authority and the ability of God were with him, to achieve God's purpose through him. And it is with this in mind that we must also refer this to our own lives.

The grace of God and the gift of God go hand in hand. His authority and His ability work together. Continually through scripture we witness this as the words **"gift"** and **"grace"** are always closely linked throughout the New Testament, as seen in the following scriptures:

- "Each one should use whatever **gift** he has received to serve others, faithfully administering **God's grace** in its various forms" (1 Peter 4:10)

- "To each of us **grace** has been given as Christ apportioned it" (Ephesians 4:7)

- "And **gifts** of the Holy Spirit distributed according to His will" (Hebrews 2:4)

- "Now to each one the manifestation of the Spirit is given for the common good" (1 Corinthians 12:7)

- "There are different kinds of **gifts**, but the same Spirit" (1 Corinthians 12:4)

In closing, most of the spiritual "gifts" are for the body and why they can be referred to as the body gifts. Examples of these are listed in 1 Corinthians 12:7-11. However while there are general gifts for the body, there are also specifically gifted individuals to the body (see 1 Corinthians 12: 27-31, or Ephesians 4:7-13).

In other words there are callings and gifting and then there are specific "offices" that hold a specific governing authority and ability. All as God wills it according to His master plan and His glory!

CHAPTER 8

Staying Accountable

Then, having fasted and prayed, and laid hands on them, THEY SENT THEM away. So, being sent out by the Holy Spirit, they went... (Acts 13:3-4 NKJV)

Now the emphasis here is twofold; "They sent them..." and "...sent out by the Holy Spirit." This means that to have "official" leadership you need the authentic commissioning of the Holy Spirit alongside "recognition" that is necessary from other leaders. In order to promote Paul the apostle, God used the established leadership with whom Paul had already faithfully served, during his years of testing and ministry of helps.

Some misguided folks think that they can go around saying, "I am anointed - I don't need anybody else and I don't care what they think!" This sounds impressive to some perhaps, but really it's nothing short of "stupid!" Without recognition from other leaders our own position can never be legitimized, only jeopardized.

It's vital to work together with others. Having said this, it is also normal to lose any reputation before you gain one! Losing your life, before you save it! Dying to self so that the "person" can be built before the "ministry" and the ego dissolved! Jesus had the wilderness for this process, we have a lifetime!

Nevertheless when we humble ourselves God promises to raise us up. Therefore to go any distance in leadership and gain that recognition from other leaders, this involves humility on our part. However this doesn't mean that everybody who is in leadership becomes our apostle or mentor!

No Lone Ranger

God never called anyone to be a lone ranger. We must never work alone. There may be seasons where God strips us back, to deal with our heart motives but even in the Adullam cave, David had a small crowd going on! (1 Samuel 22:1) Paul did travel alone at times but not all the time. More importantly he did not operate alone or solely under his own authority. He worked in collaboration with other recognised leaders; especially from Antioch and Jerusalem from where he was sent out.

From inception then, it's crucial to remember that it is before God AND men that we must serve. Recognition comes from God first and then from men, but not just anyone. That's why it's important that other recognised leaders recognise us before God.

Sensationalism Evaporates

Not all will of course; but there certainly should be some! Especially those who God has brought you into divine connection with. Without this, there is no lasting influence or authority. Sensationalism evaporates; yet true anointing and genuine recognition can last a lifetime.

Certainly to begin with and on a continual basis, there must be humility and submission towards others in leadership. God did not use anyone Paul was not in submission to; instead He used an established authority that had already been set up in Antioch. God will never undermine the leadership of the body of Christ just in order to raise up someone else into a position of leadership! With recognition comes appointment (ordination) by other leaders, in other words confirmation of certain leadership qualities (Acts 5:1-11; 6:1-7; Ephesians 4:11).

However, on the other side of the spectrum there are those who want to lead without first being led. Those who have no intention of ever operating in or out from a place of submission and yet expect submission wherever they go! These types of people have to assume leadership, because they have not gone the proper way. Usually in fact they have no recognition except for their own imagination! Their assumptive leadership behaviour operates something like this:

They like to have influence (where possible) straight at the top. They like to steer where they have no authority to steer. They start by infiltrating a church or group where they have had little if any input, nor developed any real relationship or invested any quality time and yet insist on airing unqualified opinions.

Even their silence suggests something! They leave people hanging, waiting, and wondering, so that even when they are absent, everyone is still thinking about them, almost possessed in their thoughts, something that ends up completely controlling. A false dependency upon their opinions develops and this is dangerous.

Intelligence Collecting

Having successfully infiltrated and gained trust they begin to draw back causing a little confusion and hurt; making others push in even harder to them. However a big characteristic, of these unauthorised leaders is that they remain very guarded and safe about their own personal lives. They only share so much as to get you interested or impressed and then they stop. They withhold information to make people feel that they have to earn their acceptance!

All the while these bogus leaders are gaining intelligence on everything and everyone else, because knowledge is power to them. Their self-preservation goes undetected at first but then it's realised that they never give anything away about themselves. They never indulge information about their own lives yet they manage to extract information from others, about *everything*, what they are doing, how and why, only to use that information to pass judgment! They use all information they can get as strategic ammunition for such times they feel threatened!

Eventually those around them feel more and more raped of information each time they enter conversation with them. They try to resist the urge to gush but always give in to the seduction, which induces the feeling of depression, like they are literally giving their lives away.

The seduction works so well because they give off the sense that they are really interested and want to know, but less is always more with these people. The less that is shared with them the better! Their genuine concern is appealing however and they usually succeed in seducing their victim.

The depth of their concern is revealed in time, especially when they use that information just to prove their theories and issue an, "I told you so..." They estimate themselves so highly and regard their opinions as law that they act out of extreme self-righteousness and pride. But they fear exposure! So they cover their tracks so carefully so that no one tells on them!

Seduction is not always Sexual

Ever met anyone like this? I am sure that you have. We all have. Seduction is not always sexual. It can be intellectual, informational; anything that makes us feel that we must have what they have. But it's very safe for them to stay aloof, watching and judging everything from the side-lines.

Endlessly analysing, assessing, criticising but never doing anything, they are too afraid to really commit to anything - that might affect their safety zone or expose them in any way. They don't ever reveal their own weaknesses - but they want to reveal everyone else's! They feel they must rescue everybody by correcting and coaching them in the things of God! When really the greatest need is theirs! They prey on the vulnerable and it's only a matter of time before the vulnerable eventually wise up!

Most importantly they cannot prove anything; they only have words! And yet they indulge in making everyone else feel like they have achieved nothing. Nothing worthy in their sight that is! Regardless of all the proof and genuine achievements!

When they do come across genuine success it challenges their theology - and they look for ways to disprove its legitimacy and prove it wrong. They bide there time, watching, analysing and waiting for leaked bits of information that they can use. After all, anyone who is not just like them must be wrong...!

Risk of Criticizing

This is absurd. Anyone can assume the role of judge; watching everything yet remaining unaffected by anything. Anyone can do this. People who do this don't want to pay their own price - they'd rather reap the benefits of the risks that others are willing to take. After all, the bible does say - watch and pray - not watch and judge. In fact if you hear someone constantly criticizing others, just ask them when they last prayed for those same people. Their reaction should say it all.

Finally all of us should be accountable to leadership - in one-way or another. This stops us getting carried away and helps make us more careful. We cannot be established alone. Submission is not harmful for us - long term it's more than healthy. Covering - keeps us from being vulnerable and open to attack from the bogus and false.

Ultimately, anyone who persistently says "No" to the Holy Spirit - is a dangerous character. Remember, the misguided always want to steer others! And fruitless people always have big opinions that only measure up to their own dreams but not to reality.

❖

CHAPTER 9

Honouring your Apostle

One of the questions that I had for many years regarding finance was in relation to *"Does a leader need to tithe the tithe?"* The answer to this is found right here in Numbers 18:26-29 where the Levite priests were commanded to pay a tithe from the tithe that they received from the people and give it to Aaron. We can call this, **"The Aaron's Tithe."**

Leaders themselves must be responsible to tithe the tithe. "Give these instructions to the Levites: When you receive from the people of Israel the tithes I have assigned as your allotment, give a tenth of the tithes you receive to the LORD...

You must present one-tenth of the tithe received from the Israelites as a sacred offering to the LORD. This is the

Lord's sacred portion, and you must present it to Aaron the priest. **Be sure to give to the LORD the best portions of the gifts given to you"** *(Numbers 18:26-29 NLT).*

Out of interest the same scripture in the Message Bible reads: "When you get the tithe from the people... you must tithe that tithe and present it as an offering to GOD. Your offerings will be treated the same as other people's gifts... This is your procedure for making offerings to GOD from all the tithes you get from the People... give God's portion from these tithes to Aaron the priest. Make sure that God's portion is the best... and holiest of everything you get" *(Numbers 18:26-29 MSG).*

The Best of the Best

And we see very clearly that the priests lived off of the tithe, something that we must be clear about in our teaching when we teach on the subject of *God's ways of Financial Increase.* Then in regard to church leadership, pastors and directors of Christian organizations or apostolic networks, the principle remains the same, that if we teach one thing and then excuse ourselves because of our preference of position - this is completely hypocritical.

Many pastors of churches give offerings *(but they don't necessarily tithe)* - for example towards the random itinerant ministry gifts that come through and minister in their churches, including towards their own structural developments and outreach projects.

Now of course these things are wonderful but it is not what God was instructing in Numbers 18:26-29; and such *gifts* are geared to sure up one's own agenda rather than giving the best and holiest to God, which is what tithing for leaders on this level is all about.

Now developing the vision that God has given us is not wrong in itself, nor is it wrong encouraging our members to give into certain projects that in turn will enhance them. And yes teaching our people to tithe and give offerings into the storehouse so that there is meat in God's house and an open heaven where they can prosper is all good. On the other hand however when you step back and look at this theory, superficially it all looks wonderful when actually it is also teetering over the trap of deception.

Church Extension needs Financing

For instance I believe that in these end times not only will there be a greater development of networking, where ministries are concerned, but also the network of spiritual fathering via the apostolic ministry. It's important to remain connected, committed and under the right structural covering. Every leader or pastor needs to be in a relationship that is accountable in an apostolic way.

Even as an apostolic itinerant ministry myself, I can say that my wife and I are committed to other leaders that God has directed us to be accountable to, including our own pastor who is our apostolic covering.

This carries the point over that not only are our individual members called to be responsible through their connection with their local church and with their leadership, but we as ministers also must experience connectedness with the wider body and specifically apostolically, because essentially the life flow of God's anointing and blessing comes so richly and through these avenues of: connectedness, apostolic relationship and unity *(Psalm 133:1, 3)*.

And while it's important to teach our people all about tithing we also, as organizational leaders, ministries ought to be tithing faithfully to God through "tithing the tithe" to those whom God has specifically connected us to apostolically speaking.

As leaders we are not "exempt" from tithing, rather we should be "exemplary" in it by giving tithe to the "Aaron" that God has specifically placed in our lives.

So... this is where we place the tithe of the tithe - not to random itinerant ministries or events *(that flow in and out of our lives without accountability)*. When we tithe in a correct manner, we are tithing the best of the best "unto the Lord." And to this you might say, "well I'm connected and in relationship with so many!" While this might be correct, ask yourself, of all those you are "connected" to **who is your apostle?**

The Best and Holiest

Who has been assigned to be an Aaron in your life? This is something that has to be settled between you and God and not something you can change or rearrange, *(like the goal posts)* when it suits you! Again the question has to be asked, "Whom do you ultimately submit to besides the Lord? And

74

who represents God in your life? Who can speak for Him when you are not seeing straight?"

We are discussing a certain figure in your life who goes beyond mere acquaintance or friendship; someone who has a "voice" into your life, a voice that holds considerable weight when it really matters. Whoever that person is, this then is where you should be tithing your tithe *(the best and holiest part of everything given to you...v29)* to honour the Lord. And I don't mean your wage; I mean 10% of the income of the WHOLE of your ministry or church. Re-read Numbers where it says "the best of everything."

I stress, this is not an idea of mine that I have stumbled across, nor is it an effort to conjure up finances for my own ministry. As much as I relish the support that we so need, I am rather forced to correct an "incorrectness" that exists in the body by addressing this subject and using very clear scriptural instruction to do so, that is very often swept under a religious and proverbial carpet.

Don't sidestep your Responsibility

We often conveniently sidestep such issues especially those that threaten our personal economy and create a levy upon our finances!

But if we will obey scripture on this point, then this will not only release an open heaven over our personal lives as ministers but will flow down through every branch of our vision *(it is our tithe that opens up the floodgate)*. And then of course our offerings that go to those random itinerant ministries on occasion, can still bring a harvest of supply to our ministries and churches that will positively affect all of our people and only then will we be living what we teach.

Let me say, that during my travels over many years, I discovered that many pastors possess the attitude, that their own ministries are the only ones within the church that should receive a *wage* or the tithe of the tithe. However let me ask, *"IS THIS GOD'S WAY?"* I don't believe it is.

Simply because now we have various *gifts* starting churches - just to *finance* their ministries! They play the role of a pastor, with the notion that this is the only way to fund their true ministry identity. People have hidden behind the safe title of "pastor" for generations, because it is unassuming and less offensive. Nevertheless it is unscriptural for *everyone* to relinquish their true identities and callings within the body, in order to become pastors.

Restoration and Revelation

It's ludicrous and only with a restoration of all-things-apostolic can these haphazard notions be lifted. It has caused internal restrictions within the body of Christ, not allowing gifts to function as they truly should and as God designed to best benefit the whole church.

Clearly then what is really needed is a return towards the apostolic and apostolic teams working together within the body, where all gifts are recognized and can enhance one another to create a balanced fivefold ministry for its people. With a financial structure capable of supporting them with regular income and causing each *gift* to thrive and not just *survive* in the wrong position.

God has made every provision for us to be successful and to remain so. My ministry motto has always been; **"His voice is all the provision you need."** Because every instruction we need is right within His word. If we fall short, it is only when we negate on that word or fail to obey it!

❖

CHAPTER 10

God in Three-Perfect Deity

For all those who are preparing for ministry and ordination it's important to have a clear understanding of the God we serve.

But first of all let me say that all Christians can enjoy the presence of the Holy Spirit in their lives from the moment they accept Jesus Christ as Saviour. Remembering that our new birth experience *(salvation)* brings about a remedy for the condition of man.

For God so loved the world that he gave his one and only Son, Jesus.

(John 3:16)

For His purpose is that all of mankind may have eternal life, a relationship with the living God whose desire it is that we may have the fullness of the Spirit. To bring this about

Jesus tells us that no one can see the kingdom of God unless he is born-again *(John 3:3-7)*. He goes on to explain this experience by stating that flesh gives birth to flesh, but the spirit gives birth to spirit. This happens when we hear the word of truth, the gospel of our salvation:

> *You however, are controlled not by the sinful nature but by the Spirit, if the Spirit of God lives in you. And if anyone does not have the Spirit of Christ, he does not belong to Christ.*
>
> *...But if by the Spirit you put to death the misdeeds of the body, you will live, because those who are led by the Spirit of God, are sons of God.*
>
> *The Spirit himself testifies with our spirits that we are God's children.*
>
> *(Romans 8:9, 13-14, 16)*

From this, we see that the Holy Spirit indwells the human spirit at the time of salvation. We can categorise this by saying or stating this to be the *"Baptism into the Body"* i.e., *"The Body of Christ"* or the *"First Baptism."*

The Second Baptism is of course *"Water Baptism"* an outward confession of what has happened within, a symbol that we are cleansed or washed clean by the blood of the Lamb, Jesus, and His word, *(Acts 22:16; Revelation 1:5; John 15:3)*.

But then we see quite clearly that the rest of our body has to be brought into obedience. This is a lifetime event, for we are to put off the old self and put on the new *(Colossians 3:5-17)*.

Jesus taught that salvation could not be achieved by a person's own effort, self-improvement or religious celebrations. Rather it takes place when God brings about rebirth at the centre of a person's being; something new must happen.

Paul Yonggi Cho says "Think of it this way: However well a monkey imitates man, it cannot become a human being because monkeys are fundamentally different from humans in the level of their existence" (Cho 98).

John 1:13 declares that to become children of God we must be born of God: *"Which were born, not of blood, nor of the will of the flesh, nor of the will of man, but of God."*

An Outward Confession

What then does it mean that God enables sinners to be born again by water and the Holy Spirit? It is said that some people think that being born of water means physical baptism of water. But as we have already discovered that water baptism is an outward confession of what has happened within, simply a sign, a command, and a symbol.

Jesus clarifies this to Nicodemus in John 3:5,

> *Jesus answered, "I tell you the truth, no one can enter the kingdom of God unless he is born of <u>water</u> and the Spirit. Flesh gives birth to flesh, but the Spirit gives birth to the Spirit. You should not be surprised at my saying, 'You must be born again.' The wind blows wherever it pleases. You hear its sound, but you cannot tell where it comes from or where it is going. So it is with everyone born of the Spirit."*

The word *"water"* here in the scripture, above all means, *"washing."* The teaching of the bible elsewhere says, that we are washed by the word of God. Jesus said to His disciples, *"Now ye are clean through the word which I have spoken unto you" (John 15:3 KJV).* *"Now,"* not *"you are going to be,"* so the cleanliness referred to here was a present experience before the cross and before Pentecost.

Paul wrote,

> *That he might sanctify and cleanse it [the Church] with the washing of water by the word.*
>
> *(Ephesians 5:26 KJV)*

When Jesus says we must be *"born of water and of the Spirit,"* He is referring to the word of God and the Holy Spirit. Who could be the word of God but Jesus Himself?

> *The Word became flesh and made his dwelling among us. We have seen His glory, the glory of the One and Only, who came from the father, full of grace and truth.*
>
> *(John 1:14)*

Only the precious blood of Jesus, who is the living word, can make us clean – and that blood is the very word, which cleanses us.

But Jesus said we are born again *"of water"* – or the word – *"and the Spirit."* Then what does the Holy Spirit do? Ezekiel 36:26 describes beautifully how sinners are changed into new creatures by the Spirit of God:

> *A new heart also will I give you, and a new spirit will I put within you: and I will take away the stony heart out of*

82

your flesh and I will give you an heart of flesh.
(see also Ezekiel 11:19)

Today our Saviour Jesus Christ can neither be understood nor explained except through the Holy Spirit, the author of miracles and of salvation. He is the administrative agent of God's salvation, reproving us of our sin through the word and revealing Christ, who becomes our righteousness and declares the judgement to Satan:

When he comes, he will convict the world of guilt in regard to sin and righteousness and judgement.
(John 16:8 AMP)

In John 16:14, Jesus showed that He revealed Himself only through the vessel of the Holy Spirit: *"He shall glorify me: for he shall receive of mine, and shall show it unto you."*

"The Holy Spirit carries out the new creative work that transforms a person by leading him to receive eternal life and the nature of God. But the Holy Spirit goes a step beyond regeneration, and that's what the baptism of the Holy Spirit is all about."

Regeneration or Baptism

Dr. Cho goes on to say, "Regeneration is not the same experience as the baptism of *(or with)* the Holy Spirit. Of course, both regeneration and the baptism of the Holy Spirit can happen at the same time. But in other cases there is an interval of time between the two experiences" (Cho 100).

Before we take a biblical look at the difference between regeneration and the baptism of the Holy Spirit, we need to make it clear for those who may not understand the characteristics of God, that He is not three gods but **ONE GOD** who manifests Himself as **Triune.**

GOD Revealed in JESUS CHRIST

When a scribe asked Jesus to outline the chief commandment in the law, He answered, *"The most important one is this: hear, O Israel, the Lord our God, the Lord is one" (Mark 12:29)*, to which the teacher of the law replied: "Well said, teacher, you are right in saying that God is One and there is no other but Him" *(v32)*.

Ulf Ekman the founder of Word of Life Church, in Uppsala, Sweden, says, "We live in days when the Christian message is increasingly diluted and twisted. Ancient Judeo-Christian values are no longer the unquestioned norms of modern secular society, and even queried by some church leaders. Today it is vital to clearly establish, defend and uphold fundamental Christian truth and our genuine spiritual heritage."

On speaking of the triune God, Ulf Ekman says that, "God steps out of glory and manifests His unity, His eternal nature and omnipotence by means of revelation. All His other characteristics stem from these three, so that we can see, understand, love and obey Him. His personality is first outlined in the scriptures and then summarised and made plain in the incarnation of His Son, Jesus Christ" (Ekman 42).

In Hebrews 1:3, we read that Jesus is the radiance of God's glory and the exact representation of His being. So we see that God steps out of eternity into full view through:

- Representations and outlines of Himself in nature

- Revelation in the scriptures

- His Son, Jesus Christ, the image of the invisible God *(Colossians 1:15)*, in whom all the fullness of the Deity lives in bodily form *(Colossians 2:9)*

- Nowhere can we find a clearer image, a better understanding and a closer communion with God than in Christ Jesus!

A Triune GOD

Now that God appears in all His majesty, He appears as the only God and as the one God, a unity.

Exodus 20:2-3 says:

I am the Lord your God, who brought you out of Egypt, out of the land of slavery. You shall have no other gods before me.

Pastor Ekman goes on to say, **"God is one!** Yet the New Testament refers to Him **as Triune,** which has caused difficulties for many. Some evade the question of the Trinity, others try to explain it away and still others deny it. But none of these responses is necessary. We do not need to grasp everything through our intellect; we need only to accept the plain, unambiguous testimony of scripture that **God is simultaneously ONE and THREE.** He is not three gods but **One God who manifests Himself as triune."**

85

Jesus emphasises this in the Great Commission:

> ...*baptising them in the name of the Father and of the Son and of the Holy Spirit...*
>
> *(Matthew 28:19)*

"So we see that **GOD IS ONE**, yet reveals Himself in three persons. Each of these three persons is *Individually Eternal and Omnipotent,* while UNITED IN ONE SINGLE DEITY. They share one being, one will and the same characteristics while, within the Deity, they have distinct roles. Man's limited intellect cannot comprehend a God who is simultaneously one indivisible being and yet three persons. This has led to countless doctrinal arguments about the Trinity and various descriptions of the Godhead" (Ekman 44).

No matter what people think, the bible teaches that God is a triune being. For instance, Paul says in 2 Corinthians 13:14; "May the grace of the Lord Jesus Christ, and the love of God and the fellowship of the Holy Spirit be with you all."

We have another example when Jesus says; *"I and the Father are one...anyone who has seen me has seen the Father"* *(John 10:30; 14:9).* And in 1 John 2:23 He says, *"No one who denies the Son has the Father; whoever acknowledges the Son has the Father also."*

One FATHER, one SON, one HOLY SPIRIT

Since the time of the early church, the bible's teaching on the Trinity is nowhere better described than in the Athanasian Creed:

...we worship one God in Trinity and the Trinity in Unity; Neither confusing the Persons nor dividing the substance... For like as we are compelled by the Christian verity: to confess each Person by himself to be both God and Lord; so we are forbidden by the Catholic (read, Universal) Religion: to speak of three Gods or three Lords.

The Father is made of none: not created, nor begotten. The Son is of the father alone: not made, nor created, but begotten.

The Holy Ghost is of the Father and the Son: not made, nor created, nor begotten, but proceeding.

There is therefore one Father, not three Fathers; one Son, not three Sons; one Holy Ghost, not three Holy Ghosts.

And in this Trinity there is no before or after: not greater or less.

But all three Persons are co-eternal together: and co-equal. So that in all ways, as is aforesaid: both the Trinity is to be worshipped in Unity and the Unity in Trinity.

Mr. Ekman in his summary says, "The only, invisible, eternal, omnipotent God reveals Himself so that man can understand Him, communicate with Him, receive from Him and follow Him. He does all this through the scriptures and in Christ.

Some feminist-theologians strongly object to God being called the 'Father.' God's being does not comprise both the masculine and the feminine and when God created humankind in His image, He included both man and woman.

Nevertheless, the bible expressly calls God *'Our Father,'* and *'Lord'* and Jesus talked about his **'Father.'** To call God, *'Mother'* is not only utter blasphemy and gross misuse of scripture, but tantamount to replacing the God of the bible with a New Age deity" (Ekman 45).

❖

CHAPTER 11

Baptism of the Holy Spirit

Now we have an understanding of the characteristics of God, we can now move on and look at the difference between regeneration and the baptism of the Holy Spirit. Jesus promised power to all believers through the Holy Spirit after He had ascended:

> *But you will receive power when the Holy Spirit comes on you; and you will be my witnesses in Jerusalem, and in all Judea and Samaria, and to the ends of the earth.*
>
> *(Acts 1:8)*

He did not say "some of you, one or two of you, those who have specialist ministries," He said "All! All!" We exercise this power out of our position being adopted into God's family, with all the right of a child of God.

Dr. Martyn Lloyd-Jones says when writing in the Westminster Record in September 1964:

"There is nothing, I am convinced, that so quenches the Spirit as the teaching which identifies the baptism of the Holy Spirit with regeneration, but it is a very commonly held teaching today, indeed it has been the popular view for many years.

They say that the baptism of the Holy Spirit is *'non-experimental,'* that it happens to everybody at regeneration. So we say 'ah-well, I am already baptised in the Holy Spirit, it happened when I was born again, it happened at my conversion; there is nothing for me to seek, I have got it all.'

Got it all? Well, if you have got it all, I simply ask in the name of God why are you as you are? If you have got it all, why are you so unlike those apostles, why are you unlike New Testament Christians? Got it all! Got it all at your conversion! Well, where is it I ask."

Baptism or Infilling

In the bible there is clear mention of born-again believers who had not received the baptism or infilling with the Holy Spirit. For instance the Old Testament saints had many experiences and blessing, as follows:

They were *filled* (*Exodus 28:3; 31:3; 35:31; Deuteronomy 34:9; Micah 3:8*) and had the Spirit *in* (*Genesis 41:38; Numbers 27:18; Daniel 4:8-9, 18; 5:11-14; 6:3*); *within* (*Psalms 51:10-11; Isaiah 63:10-14; Ezekiel 11:19*); *into* (*Ezekiel 2:2; 3:24; Acts 3:21*);

upon *(Numbers 11:17-29; Judges 3:10; 6:34; 11:29; 14:6, 19; 15:14)*; and He *moved* many *(Judges 13:25; Acts 3:21; 2 Peter 1:21)*, but none were baptised in the Spirit.

John the Baptist and others were filled with the Spirit, but not baptised *(Luke 1:15-17, 41, 67; 2:25-38)*. Mary was filled about 35 years before she was baptised with the Holy Spirit at Pentecost and spoke in Tongues *(Luke 1:46-56; Acts 1:13-15, 2:1-4)*. Jesus was filled about 30 years before He was baptised with the Spirit *(Isaiah 50:4-5; Luke 2:40-52; Matthew 3:16-17)*. The disciples were filled and had the Spirit in them 3 years before they were baptised with the Spirit *(Matthew 10:8, 20; Acts 1:4-8; 2:1-4, 23)*.

Before Jesus' death His disciples had already received eternal life, for Jesus called them in person and they obeyed Him, believing that He was the Son of God.

Jesus said, "Verily, verily, I say unto you, He that heareth my word, and believeth on him that sent me, hath everlasting life."

(John 5:24 KJV)

Jesus also testified in John 13:10 that His disciples were all clean except Judas Iscariot. And when the seventy disciples returned from preaching and told Jesus how the devils were subject to them, Jesus admitted that the seventy disciples had already received everlasting life *(see Luke 10:20)*. But Jesus did not say that they had received the baptism of the Holy Spirit from the moment they believed, as some theologians today claim.

It's quite clear that they hadn't yet received the fullness of the Spirit. Before He ascended into heaven, Jesus told His disciples that they should not depart from Jerusalem yet:

Wait for the promise of the Father, which ye have heard of me. For John truly baptised with water; but ye shall be baptised with the Holy Ghost not many days hence.
(Acts 1:4, 5 KJV)

Some people agree that the believing disciples needed the baptism of the Holy Spirit, but they say, that was only because they were believers before Pentecost. The argument goes that any believer since Pentecost, when the church was born and the Holy Spirit descended, received the baptism of the Holy Spirit at this time of conversion. But New Testament accounts show such a theory to be wrong.

Distinctions

The distinction between being born again *(conversion)* and the baptism with the Holy Spirit can be seen in the accounts of this manifestation recorded in the book of Acts. On numerous occasions, believers were prayed for to receive the baptism or infilling with the Holy Spirit, after they had been converted.

In Acts 8:4-24 we can see that the gospel was being preached by Philip in Samaria. The people there "with one accord gave heed unto those things which Philip spake, hearing and seeing the miracles which he did" (KJV). As a result, "…unclean spirits, crying with loud voice, came out of many that were possessed with them: and many taken with palsies and that were lame, were healed. And there was great joy in that city" (KJV).

Those who believed what Philip was preaching were baptised in water, a sign of a person's entrance into the body of Christ. Jesus had said, *"He who has believed and has been baptised shall be saved" (Mark 16:16 NASB)*. Thus, these Samaritans were saved, members of the body of Christ, and *"there was much rejoicing in that city" (Acts 8:8 NASB)*. And yet, they had not yet received the infilling of the Spirit. *"For He (the Spirit) had not yet fallen on any of them" (Acts 8:16 NASB)*.

Not one of the Same

We can see from this passage that the new birth and the baptism in the Holy Spirit are not one and the same. The Samaritans were born again *(saved)* when they *"received the word of God" (Acts 8:14 NASB)*. But, this did not automatically give them the infilling of the Holy Spirit, that manifestation came when the apostles laid hands on them.

> *Now when the apostles which were at Jerusalem heard that Samaria had received the word of God, they sent unto them Peter and John: Who, when they were come down, prayed for them, that they might receive the Holy Ghost: (For as yet he was fallen upon none of them: only they were baptised in the name of the Lord Jesus.) Then laid they their hands on them, and they received the Holy Ghost.*
>
> *(Acts 8:14-17 KJV)*

Again in Acts 9:1-19 we see another distinction where Paul tells a vivid account of his conversion and experience of being filled with the Holy Spirit, which didn't happen simultaneously.

With a letter of authority from the high priests, Saul and his friends went toward Damascus, the capital of Syria, to persecute those who believed in Jesus and bring them into prison. But when he and his followers came near Damascus, *"suddenly there shined round about him a light from heaven"* which blinded him.

This new birth is evidence by the fact that he addressed the risen Christ as *"Lord" (Acts 9:5)*, and then asked Jesus what He wanted him to do *(Acts 22:10)* and obeyed Him. Saul subsequently called Paul, said later that this was his witness of the resurrection *(1 Corinthians 15:8)*.

The man who was led blind into the city of Damascus was a man who had witnessed and believed in the resurrected Christ and had submitted himself to His Lordship. Saul fasted and prayed for three days. From this we see that he has become a new creature in Christ. Then Ananias put his hands on Saul and prayed that he be filled with the Holy Spirit, which he was.

Struggling is a Sign

"Another example is the church at Ephesus, which had been established through the eloquent preaching of Apollos. But when Paul visited that Church, he found it struggling and weak. The first question Paul asked was this: *'Have ye received the Holy Ghost since ye believe?' (Acts 19:2 KJV)* Paul knew that if they had received the Holy Spirit, they wouldn't have been so powerless and feeble with only twelve or so members.

If Christians always received the Holy Spirit when they believed, why would Paul have deliberately asked the unnecessary question, *'Have ye received the Holy Ghost since ye believed?'* Faith does not mean that one automatically receives the fullness of the Holy Spirit. It is something a believer should pray and ask for.

I'm not saying that one cannot be saved and filled with the Holy Spirit at the same time. Cornelius and his household had the Holy Spirit fall upon them as they were listening to Peter preach. No appeal was made to Cornelius to repent or confess; the Spirit fell upon him as he believed what Peter was saying about the Lord Jesus *(Acts 10:44)*.

However, this does not mean that those two works of God are one and the same. If that were the case, the Samaritans *(who had received the word and been baptised in water)* would not have needed to afterward receive the Spirit. If being born again meant the same thing as being filled with the Spirit, the convert Saul would not have needed Ananias to lay his hands on him to be filled with the Holy Spirit.

A Necessary Qualification

In fact, first-century Spirit-filled believers thought that Christians who weren't Spirit-filled lacked a necessary qualification for service. Because of this, new believers as a rule prayed earnestly to receive the Holy Spirit. Before the believers at Ephesus received the Holy Spirit, the church was miserably weak and sick. But after the people received the fullness of the Holy Spirit through Paul's ministry, a wonderful vitality and power of faith exploded in their midst. After a while it became a famous church that filled all of Asia Minor with the word of God.

When we take all these accounts into consideration, we can see that regeneration and the baptism with the Holy Spirit are two distinctly different experiences. Regeneration is the experience of receiving the life of the Lord by being grafted into the body of Christ through the Holy Spirit and the scriptures. The baptism of the Holy Spirit is the experience in which Jesus fills believers with the power of God for ministry, service and victorious living.

Regeneration Grants a Person Everlasting Life

While the baptism of the Holy Spirit grants regenerated believers the power of God to preach Christ. Christians today are not powerless, sick and spiritless because they are not born again, but because they have not received the fullness of the Holy Spirit, the tremendous power of God for service.

Without the baptism of the Holy Spirit the church today can never display God's power as did the early church – a combative, challenging and victorious power to evangelise a generation. For this reason, we should renounce the foolish, weak and lethargic excuse that all believers immediately receive the Holy Spirit when they believe. Rather we should pray to receive the fullness of the Holy Spirit" (Cho 103).

Old Testament saints had gifts and fruit of the Spirit (*1 Kings 3:12; 17:1; 2 Kings 13:25; Acts 3:21; Hebrews 11*); different measures of the Spirit (*Numbers 11:16-25; 2 Kings 2:9; Luke 1:17*) but not the Spirit baptism or the Spirit *"without measure"* (*John 3:34; 7:37-39*). The disciples had gifts and great power years before the Spirit baptism *(Matthew 10:1-8, 16-20; Mark 6:7-13; Luke 10),* but were told to get the Spirit baptism before starting their ministry *(Luke 24:49; John 7:37-39; 14:12; Acts 1:4-8).*

Saints and disciples of Christ had salvation *(Psalms 51:12);* **redemption** *(Psalms 31:5);* **grace** *(Psalms 84:11);* **bodily healing** *(Exodus 15:26);* **names written in heaven** *(Exodus 32:32-33; Luke 10:20);* **the new birth** *(Galatians 4:28-30);* **conversion** *(Psalms 19:7);* **righteousness** *(Romans 4);* **the gospel** *(Galatians 3:6-14; Hebrews 4:2);* **justification** *(Romans 4);* **holiness** *(Acts 3:21: 2 Peter 1:21);* **pure hearts** *(Psalms 24:4);* **sanctification** *(Exodus 29:42-44; 31:13; Ezekiel 20:12; John 15:3);* **and many other spiritual blessings before Pentecost** *(John 7:37-39; Acts 2:33).*

Therefore, one should **not take any of these blessings as evidence of a Spirit baptism.** From all this we gather that the Spirit baptism is the fullness of God in the lives of believers, not the Spirit by measure as in OT times *(John 3:34; 7:37-39; Luke 24:49; Acts 10:38; Isaiah 61:1; Romans 15:29; Ephesians 3:19).*

The late Bob Gordon said, "If the Lord Jesus needed to be filled *(Luke 4:1, 14),* the apostles needed to be filled *(Acts 2:2-4),* and Paul needed to be filled *(Acts 9:17),* we also need to be filled with the Holy Spirit.

Deposit or Baptism

This is not simply becoming a Christian and receiving the Holy Spirit as a deposit guaranteeing our salvation *(Ephesians 1:13-14).* Jesus was conceived by the Holy Spirit

(Matthew 1:18), and so has the Holy Spirit in Him all His life, but He still needed to be filled or baptised with the Holy Spirit in order to fulfil all that His Father had sent Him to do.

This happened when He was baptised in water at the river Jordan *(Luke 3:21-22).* The disciples received the Holy Spirit when Jesus breathed on them *(John 20:22),* but they were told to wait until they had received the baptism with the Holy Spirit before they began their ministry *(Acts 1:4-5; 2:2-4).*

The bible uses many different ways to describe this filling. These include being filled *(Acts 2:4);* being baptised *(Acts 1:5);* the Holy Spirit coming upon *(Acts1:8);* receiving the Holy Spirit *(Acts 8:17);* pouring out of the Holy Spirit *(Acts 10:45).* It is not the label that matters but what actually happens, that is, we are enabled to do God's will and to be true disciples of our Lord Jesus Christ" (Gordon and Fardouly 47).

It must be remembered that we are not just to be filled once and leave it at that. **We need to be CONTINUALLY FILLED WITH THE HOLY SPIRIT** *(Ephesians 5:18; Acts 2:1-4; 4:31).*

❖

CHAPTER 12

New Days – New Ways

They dress the wound of my people as though it were not serious. "Peace, peace," they say, when there is no peace (Jeremiah 6:14).

In this final chapter we will cover an interesting topic, especially considering current events, involving such figureheads as the Pope and the Catholic Church. However from the outset let me clarify that currently my wife and I are living in Tuscany, Italy *(even though we have offices in other parts of the world)* and I have preached more than once in Catholic churches here, whom I have always found to be open if not more-open-and-hungry for the things of God than other churches I experience!

For instance, there have been the occasions that I have gone up to preach for Padre Don Stefano, who lived on top of a mountain here in Tuscany - and have enjoyed some spectacular events with him *(a mountain that takes roughly two and a half hours to ascend - even with a car!)*

The precise reason that he was placed there was due to his sincere belief in the things of the Holy Spirit. Something that his peers in the Catholic Church did not collectively appreciate some decades before and decidedly put-him-out-to-graze in order to minimize the influence of his beliefs on others. In other words, his own church effectively ostracized him in an attempt to quench the Holy Spirit's fire.

No one can Stop You

However as it stats in John 12:32, if Jesus is lifted up, all men will be drawn to Him. Therefore we know and have confidence that the Holy Spirit will always find a way to draw people unto Christ. Despite all their efforts, those in the hierarchy in the Catholic Church were unable to hinder the moving of the Holy Spirit for long, as Padre Don Stefano regularly attracts hundreds upon hundreds to his meetings on the mountain top.

Many came via the coach load *(totally disregarding the difficulty of logistics!)* especially for such calendar events as "Pentecost," where typically Don Stefano would invite known "Pentecostals" to come and preach for him on those specific occasions - which is where I came in of course!

So as you can tell, I have always and will always preach where the doors are open and where I feel the leading of God's Spirit, whom over the years I have discovered, will transcend any humanistic boundary and anoint me to preach right across the board; with strong love without ever compromising the scriptures.

So having said all this - by way of small disclaimer - nothing changes the fact that there are obvious discrepancies within the doctrine of the Catholic Church! Yet with nothing posing too great of a challenge or a threat for the Holy Spirit - keeping this in mind - let us read on, from this excerpt taken from my own book material on the End Times - entitled, **"Israel, The Church And The End Times."**

It was interesting that several years ago, Archbishop Runcie who was the head of the Church of England, told *"Time Magazine"* that he had given a ring to Pope John Paul II as *"an engagement ring"* in view of the coming marriage between the Roman Catholic Church and the Church of England.

What Ecumenical Union?

Remember the Church of Rome has not renounced any of the fundamental doctrinal errors that provoked the Protestant Reformation in AD 1520. **The non-Catholic members of the union are making this Ecumenical union on the basis of theological compromise.**

Even Catholic theologians admit that John Paul II was the most traditional Pope of this last century and the strongest advocate of worship of Mary, Queen of Heaven, Mother of God, as the *"co-redenitrix"* along with Jesus Christ. However a process of intense ecumenical dialogue has proceeded quietly during the last twenty years or so! The church leaders are very close to healing the schism between the Greek and Russian Orthodox Churches and the Church of Rome. The Pope has met with Buddhist, Muslim, and Jewish religious leaders from around the world.

For the first time in history the Vatican has sought to establish ties with those other churches. He has engaged in ecumenical religious rituals and services with other religions that would have been unimaginable for any previous Pope.

The danger today is that in opting for a man-made unity based on compromise; and abandoning the Protestant Reformation and the truths of the scriptures that were sealed in the blood of martyrs, we are heading back to whence we came.

Love is not always Truth

Michael de Semlyen says, today in Britain, there is a *"love gospel"* about, which confines itself exclusively to what is called *"the positive."* It is claimed that as long as Jesus Christ is proclaimed as Saviour and Lord, we are all as one in Him. Differences over doctrine must not be allowed to get in the way of this. They say, **"we can affirm truth, but not confront error!"**

Even Evangelical Alliance, UK Director *(at the time)*, Clive Calver said: "More barriers need to come down if a true alliance of evangelicals in the UK is to emerge. There are thousands more with whom we wish to stand shoulder to shoulder." Is this part of the New World Order? It must be said that those who are pointing the finger and accusing many whom are standing for truth, as "SECTS," are very often part of the so-called unity at any cost; which is part of the Babylonian church!

A.W. Tozer said, "Every century needs its prophetic voices. Those men who have been gifted by God with an incisive cutting edge to expose hypocrisy, denounce compromise, and call for holiness."

He also said, "If THE CHURCH in the second half of this century is to recover from the injuries which she suffered in the first half, there must appear a new type of preacher. The proper ruler of the synagogue type will never do. Neither will the priestly type of man who carries out his duties, takes his pay and asks no questions, nor the smooth talking pastoral type who knows how to make the Christian religion acceptable to everyone.

All these have been tried and found wanting. Another kind of religious leader must arise among us. He must be of the old prophet type, a man who has seen visions of God and has heard a voice from the throne.

Peace at any Cost

The Protestant martyrs, godly and loving men, 'could have taken this same position of, peace at any cost, within the wider church of their day. They could have confined themselves to avoiding all controversy and to agreeing with their persecutors about many of the 'positives'. But, the scripture commanded them to 'exhort and convince by sound doctrine' and to 'flee from idolatry.'

They obeyed; they saw the error and the idolatry, and as responsible leaders, as pastors trusted to guide their flocks into green pastures, they exposed and opposed it all roundly. They could so easily have chosen to look the other way and concentrate on the many truths of the Christian faith, which was common ground. They could have elected to please men, rather than please God."

The Reformers saw the whole Catholic system as anti-Christian. Luther and Calvin went so far as to identify the Papacy with the Antichrist and they like Wycliffe, Tyndale, Matthew Henry, Spurgeon, Llyod-Jones and many others saw the Roman Catholic Institution as Mystery Babylon, the Mother of Harlots, vividly described in Revelation 17. The Spirit-filled life is filled with testimony of experience which of course is not wrong in itself, but **"New Days, New Ways"** is a dangerous way of life!

A New Cross

"I well knew how many smooth arguments can be marshalled in support of the new cross," says A.W. Tozer. Does not the new cross win converts and make many followers and so carry the advantage of numerical success? **Should we not adjust ourselves to the changing times?** Have we not heard the slogan, *"New days, New ways?"* And who but someone very old and very conservative would insist upon death as the appointed way to life? And who today is interested in a gloomy mysticism that would sentence its flesh to a cross and recommend self-effacing humility as a virtue actually to be practised by modern Christians?

These are the arguments along with many more flippant still, which are brought forward to give an appearance of wisdom to the hollow and meaningless cross of popular Christianity.

He says (Tozer) "Doubtless there are many whose eyes are open to the tragedy of our times, but why are they so silent when their testimony is so sorely needed. **In the name of Christ men have made void the cross of Christ.**

'The noise of them that sing do I hear.' Men have fashioned a golden cross with a graving tool, and before it they sit down to eat and drink and rise up to play. In their blindness they have substituted the work of their own hands for the working of God's power. Perhaps our greatest present need may be the coming of a prophet to dash the stones at the foot of the mountain and call the Church out to repentance or to judgment.

Please Lord send a Prophet

Before all who wish to follow Christ the way lies clear. It is the way of death unto life. Always life stands just beyond death and beckons the man who is sick of himself to come and know the life more abundant. But to reach the new life he must pass through the valley of the shadow of death, and I know that at the sound of those words many will turn back and follow Christ no more. But to whom shall we go? 'Thou hast the words of eternal life.'"

To close, let us be mindful of all that has been brought out in this book, "The Age of Apostolic Apostleship"

105

Preparations for Ministry (Part Three), and resist becoming part of a false "Doctrine," whether Catholic, Anglican, Protestant or Pentecostal that cries peace when there is no peace! (Jeremiah 6:14) For those of us who entered into the life of Christ, we chose to be identified as such; an identity that we cannot afford to compromise.

In fact we live in a day where the distinctions are becoming more and more acute - in the context that the dark is getting darker and the brightness is getting brighter! In other words the dividing lines, although fudged, for many are still strong. We must make our daily choices wisely and never lean back into deception.

Let us therefore not be fearful of hearing the voice of God's prophets. Satan has undermined the authority of the apostolic and prophet in every generation, including this one - simply because they threaten him the most!

Remember that God Himself singles them out when He declares, "Come not against Mine anointed ones, and against My prophets do not evil" *(1 Chronicles 16:22 YLT)*. They will always be singled-out so we must not be timid about them. Instead let us become a generation that develops ears to hear the voice of His prophets - resisting our human instinct that despises this gift.

They may not be as smooth talking as the other gifts, even much less articulate perhaps especially to the humanistic crowd; but oh how we need this potent gift in the body of Christ today! Amen.

❖
Bibliography

- Cho, Paul Y. The Holy Spirit My Senior Partner. Copyright © 1989. Published by Charismas Media. Printed in USA.

- Ekman, Ulf. Doctrine. Copyright © 1996. Published by Word of Life Publications. Printed in Sweden.

- Gordon, Bob, and David Fardouly. The Foundations of Christian Living. Copyright © 1988. Published by Sovereign World. Printed in England.

- Strong, James. S.T.D., L.L.D. 1890. Strong's Exhaustive Concordance; Dictionaries of the Hebrew and Greek Words. e-Sword ® version 7.6.1 Copyright © 2000-2005. All Rights Reserved. Registered trade mark of Rick Meyers. Equipping Ministries Foundation. USA www.e-sword.net.

- Tozer, A.W. The Divine Conquest. Copyright © 1995. Published by Living Books. Printed in USA.

- Unless otherwise indicated, all scriptural quotations are from the HOLY BIBLE, NEW INTERNATIONAL VERSION ®. NIV ®. Copyright © 1973, 1978, 1984 by the International Bible Society. Used by permission of Zondervan Publishing House. All rights reserved.

- Scripture references marked AMP are taken from The Amplified Bible. Old Testament copyright © 1965, 1987 by Zondervan Corporation, Grand Rapids, Michigan. New Testament copyright © 1958, 1987 by The Lockman Foundation, La Habra, California. All rights reserved.

- Scripture references marked GW are taken from GOD'S WORD®, © 1995 God's Word to the Nations. Used by permission of Baker Publishing Group.

- Scripture references marked KJV are taken from the King James Version of the bible.

- Scripture references marked MSG are taken from The Message. Copyright © 1993, 1994, 1995, 1996, 2000, 2001, 2002. Used by permission of NavPress Publishing Group.

- Scripture references marked NASB are taken from New American Standard Bible®, Copyright © 1960, 1962, 1963, 1968, 1971, 1972, 1973, 1975, 1977, 1995 by The Lockman Foundation. Used by permission.

- Scripture references marked NKJV are taken from the New King James Version. Copyright © 1982 by Thomas Nelson, 1982 by Thomas Nelson, Inc. Used by permission. All rights reserved.

- Scripture references marked NLT are taken from the Holy Bible, New Living Translation, copyright © 1996, 2004, 2007 by Tyndale House Foundation. Used by permission of Tyndale House Publishers, Inc., Carol Stream, Illinois 60188. All rights reserved.

- Scripture references marked YLT are taken from the Young's Literal Translation of the bible.

❖

Ministry Profile

Doctor Alan Pateman, an apostle, is the President and Founder of **"Alan Pateman Ministries International"** (APMI), which was established in England back in 1987, a Christian-based *(parachurch)* non-profit and non-denominational outreach. This ministry is now focusing in two main areas: First **"Connecting for Excellence"** Apostolic Networking (CFE) and secondly, the teaching arm, **"LifeStyle International Christian University"** (LICU).

CFE is a multi-facetted missions organisation with the purpose of connecting leaders for divine opportunities and building lasting relationships, to touch the lives of leaders literally the world over. Apostle Dr Alan Pateman has to date ordained more than 500 ministers in over 50 NATIONS. In addition there are ministries, churches and schools who are in Association or Affiliation, looking to him for apostolic counsel and oversight.

Secondly LICU, which was founded in 2007, is a study program to help people discover their purpose and destiny. A global network of university campuses and correspondence students, demonstrating the Supernatural Kingdom of God through Doctrinal, Apostolic and Prophetic Teaching. Dr Alan holds the position of President/CEO, Professor of Theology, Biblical Studies and Apostolic Ministry. LICU is exploding throughout Europe, Asia and Africa, enhancing the Body of Christ

Dr Alan has authored more than 35 books including numerous teaching materials and LICU university courses (30) along with hundreds of Truth for the Journey articles on kingdom lifestyle *(that are regularly distributed globally via the internet).*

He is recognised as an Apostle, Bishop, Leadership Mentor, University Educator, Motivational Speaker, Connector and Author, who has also been featured on national and international TV and radio networks throughout the years.

Currently Apostle Alan, his wife Dr Jennifer reside in Lucca *(Tuscany)* Italy and travel out from their Apostolic Company.

- Alan Pateman Ph.D., D.Min., D.D., M.A., B.Th.

Academic Background

Dr. Alan Pateman attended several colleges throughout his training *(including studying Theology at Roffey Place, Horsham, UK and a Member of Kerygma - with Rev. Colin Urquhart and Dr. Bob Gordon - 1985-1987)* before being awarded a Doctorate of Divinity *(2006)* in recognition of his lifetime achievements by the International College of Excellence, now "DanEl Christian College" *(President: Dr. Robb Thompson USA)* also "Life Christian University" *(Dr. Douglas Wingate USA)* where he also earned a Bachelor of Theology B.Th. *(2006),* a Master of Arts in Theology M.A., a Doctor of Ministry in Theology D.Min., *(2007)* and Doctor of Philosophy in Theology Ph.D. *(2013)* from LICU.

❖

To Contact the Author

Please email:

Alan Pateman Ministries International

Email: apostledr@alanpateman.com
Web: www.AlanPatemanMinistries.com

*Please include your prayer requests
and comments when you write.*

❖
Other Books

Laying Foundations (Apostleship Series) Part One

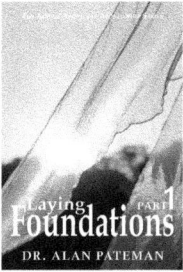

In order to view how the Apostolic baton was successfully passed from one generation to the next. Knowing that through the perseverance and obedience of others - history as we know it was altered forever. Therefore it is my desire to encourage all those that are part of Connecting for Excellence to have a solid foundation, insight and teaching that will propel them into God's divine purposes.

ISBN: 978-1-909132-56-6, Pages: 140,
Format: Paperback, Published: 2017
Also available in eBook format!

Seduction & Control:
Infiltrating Society & the Church

This book is a glance into the world of seduction and control, how they try to influence the Church through many powerful avenues such as the New Age, sexual education in our schools, basic entertainment; things that touch our everyday lives in order that we effectively and gradually become desensitised.

ISBN: 978-1-909132-00-9, Pages: 156
Format: Paperback, Published: 2015
Also available in eBook format!

Truth for the Journey Books

WINNING by Mastering your Mind

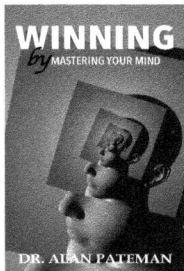

Someone once said, "Happiness begins between your ears and your mind is the drawing room for tomorrow's circumstances..." Remember, what happens in your mind will happen in time, and therefore one of our first priorities must be mind-management.

ISBN: 978-1-909132-40-5, Pages: 136,
Format: Paperback, Published: 2017
Also available in eBook format!

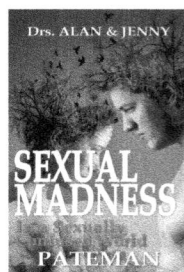

Sexual Madness: In a Sexually Confused World

This book discusses the sensitive subject of political correctness in our world today and the growing fear of causing offence in the public arena. It also discusses the rise of homosexuality, pedophilia and all other forms of sexuality, as there are many. Including modern statistics on pornography.

ISBN: 978-1-909132-02-3, Pages: 160,
Format: Paperback, Published: 2012
Also available in eBook format!

His Life is in the Blood

Blood is the trophy of every battle. The spilt blood of Jesus Christ is our trophy. It is our freedom from sin and bondage. Nothing can enter the blood-bought temples of the Holy Ghost! This book will encourage you to apply the blood of Jesus our Passover Lamb to your life, just as the children of Israel did in the Old Testament. Not merely talking or reading about it, but applying it.

ISBN: 978-1-909132-06-1, Pages: 152,
Format: Paperback, First Published: 2007
Also available in eBook format!

Dear Friends,

Have you considered becoming one of our international students? We are privileged to welcome you, from around the world, to "LifeStyle International Christian University" *(the teaching arm of Alan Pateman Ministries International).* **An English speaking university** dedicated to your success; to see you trained and equipped to fully succeed in your God given Destiny.

It is our passion to raise up the leaders of tomorrow, who will have influence in all realms of authority, including the Body of Christ. Men and women of strategy, wisdom and true godliness, who'll stand with stature and maturity in this hour.

It's undeniable that in today's world, recognised education has become indispensable, therefore it is our desire to offer well balanced and well structured courses. Those that have been written by gifted and talented ministers of God, who seek to be inspired by God's Holy Spirit.

Consequently we have put together a **flexible curriculum,** designed both for correspondence students and campuses, which is a strategy to reach the distant learner; whether provincial, national or international. In fact we have many correspondence students from around the world, including a growing number of successful campuses, in various countries.

This is a growing platform, where men and women of dignity and passion, can grow and be established in their God given endeavours. As God is the healer of the nations, we pray and believe that many of our alumni will go on to **become world changers** in their own right.

We are proud of each and every one of our LICU students.

It would be our pleasure if you would join them on this incredible journey!

Doctor Alan Pateman

Alan Pateman Prof. Ph.D., D.Min., D.D., M.A., B.Th.
PRESIDENT AND CEO
www.licuuniversity.com   www.cfeapostolicnetwork.com
Email: info@licuuniversity.com   Mob: +39 366 329 1315

For more information visit our website/facebook or contact our office, using the details below:

Website: www.licuuniversity.com
Facebook: www.facebook.com/LICUMainCampus
Email: info@licuuniversity.com
Telephone: +39 366 329 1315

Alan Pateman Ministries
Presents

Conference

CONNECTING FOR EXCELLENCE Lucca Italy

An international apostolic
and prophetic network

YOUR HOSTS: ALAN PATEMAN   JENNIFER PATEMAN

apostledr@alanpateman.com, Tel. 0039 366 329 1315

W W W . A L A N P A T E M A N M I N I S T R I E S . C O M

Please contact our office or download the registration form.
Registration fee: €40

All Books Available

at

APMI PUBLICATIONS

Email: publications@alanpateman.com
*Also Available from Amazon.com
and other retail outlets.*

*If you purchased this book through Amazon.com
or other and enjoyed reading it, or perhaps one of
my other books, I would be grateful if you could
take a couple of minutes to write a Customer
Review, many thanks.*

www.ingramcontent.com/pod-product-compliance
Lightning Source LLC
Chambersburg PA
CBHW071453070426
42452CB00039B/1228